But Mommy, I Don't Want To!

But Mommy, I Don't Want To!

Candilyn Gee & Ace Gee

Illustrated by Jonathan Zepeda

But Mommy, I Don't Want To!

Published by Gatekeeper Press

7853 Gunn Hwy., Suite 209

Tampa, FL 33626

www.GatekeeperPress.com

Library of Congress Control Number: 2023933184

ISBN (hardcover): 9781662937446

ISBN (paperback): 9781662937453

eISBN: 9781662937460

Ace had a full day of fun and play.

"Don't forget to put your toys away."

"But Mommy,
I don't want to."

"Wash from your head to your toes,

and don't forget your nose."

"But Mommy,
I don't want to."

"Your teeth need brushing.

Take your time, Ace, no rushing.

Don't forget to floss."

"But Mommy,
I don't want to."

"Wrap your hair in your favorite scarf.

When you wake, you can take it off."

"But Mommy,
I don't want to."

"Go potty before we end the night.

No accidents just how we like.

Don't forget to wipe."

"But Mommy,
I don't want to."

"Time to shut your little eyes.

Dream big, Ace, ease your mind.

Everything you do is right on time.

I'm so happy that you are mine."

"But Mommy...

"I love you SO much. Goodnight, Mom."

"I love you
more. Goodnight,
Sweetheart."

About the Authors

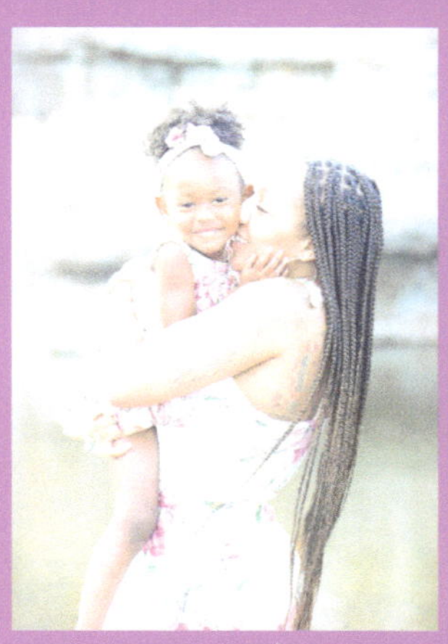 Senior Chief Petty Officer Candilyn Gee has served in the United States Navy for seventeen years. During this time, she earned her bachelor's degree in psychology and her master's degree in business administration. As a great leader and mentor, she continues to chase her career goals during the day. On her off time, she enjoys spending time with family and honing in on her childhood passion of reading and writing. Luckily, these two skills were inherited to her four-year-old daughter, Ace, who is a phenomenal storyteller with the biggest imagination. This loving mother-daughter duo is excited to welcome readers into their lives in hopes that their stories resonate with families all over the world.

# THE BRADBURY BUILDING

Sandy Bleifer

THE BRADBURY BUILDING

ISBN: 978-1-7330719-1-8
Library of Congress Control Number: 2019907967

THE BRADBURY BUILDING
A photographic essay exploring one of the most iconic buildings in downtown Los Angeles, capturing the amazing quality of light that transcends even its extraordinary architectural detail. The book is a tribute to, not only the building's namesake and architect, but to Ira Yellin, the visionary developer who engaged preservation architect, Brenda Levin, to sensitively restore a National Register Historic property and downtown's crown jewel.

Photography: Sandy Bleifer
Book Design by Michele Castagnetti / AcrylicAirlines.com

Published by Sandy Bleifer / Bleifer InPrint

www.sandybleifer.com

BRADBURY.
304
304

THE BRADBURY BUILDING
1893

The Bradbury Building, a "symphony of glazed brick, ornamental cast iron, tiling, rich marble and polished wood railings, flooded in light from the huge skylight five stories above," transcends time and continues to attract a steady stream of awestruck visitors since its restoration in 1990 by preservation architect, Brenda Levin, under the direction of visionary developer/owner, Ira Yellin. An unimposing Italian Renaissance exterior façade is deceptive, providing no indication of the transcendent experience of entering the central lobby. Built in 1893 and certified as a National Historic Landmark, the building's history is as dramatic as the architecture itself.

Lewis Bradbury was a mining millionaire turned real estate developer who, in 1892, decided to construct a five-story building at Third and Broadway. The plans developed by a well-known architect, Sumner Hunt, disappointed Mr. Bradbury who wanted something unique. Believing in the potential of an obscure draftsman, he asked 32-year old George Wyman to create a design. At first, Wyman declined the offer, but after debating the matter he decided to get advice from his brother, who was then dead for six years. The Planchette Board, a precursor to the Ouija board, was used to channel a "spirit" message that read: "Take Bradbury Building. It will make you famous."

Wyman decided to design the building based on Edward Bellamy's science fiction story, "Looking Backward" published in 1887, which described a utopian civilization in the year 2000. In the book, one of the author's imagined visions resembles the interior of the Bradbury building: "A vast hall of light received not alone from the windows on all sides but from the dome, the point of which was a hundred feet above…The walls were frescoed in mellow tints, to soften without absorbing the light which flooded the interior."

The entire area, including geometric patterned staircases at either end, is covered with ornately designed railings of wrought iron giving the illusion of hanging vegetation. The wrought iron decoration was made in France and first displayed at the Chicago World's Fair before installation in the building. Even the mail chutes are tall poles of metal not supported by any wall. The walls are pale brick and the floors are Mexican tile with imported Belgian marble used in the staircases. Such was Bradbury's desire for quality that the rich wood paneling is even carried out in the basement.

Knowing Wyman's background, it seems impossible that such an innovative, lasting design could be his. Neither an architect nor engineer, his only building experience had been a few years as a $5 a week apprentice to an architect. But a major trade magazine, "Arts and Architecture", is quick to reject the idea it was all an accident:

"There is nothing whatever accidental about it. There are no afterthoughts."

"It is a forever young building, out of a youthful and vigorous imagination. But it has left nothing to chance. Stairways leap into space because of endless calculations. The skylight is a fairy tale of mathematics."

For Wyman, the building was to be his one masterpiece.

Yet, by the mid-1940s as the city spread out to the suburbs in the post-war boom and downtown, the Bradbury and subsequent architectural gems of the 1920's fell into misuse and disrepair. It took another visionary, Ira Yellin, a lawyer cum developer who grew up in Los Angeles and was smitten early by the historic buildings of downtown, to bring the Bradbury back to life.

When Yellin heard about the possibility of the State Office Building going in on Spring Street in 1984, he thought then that the Grand Central Market could become the linkage between the old and the new downtown. Later acquiring the Million Dollar Theater with the Metropolitan Water District offices above and the Bradbury, he said, "I see Broadway as a crossroads…one of the great treasures of the City." In restoring these three historic landmarks on Broadway, he envisioned these properties becoming vital links between the past and the future and the many cultures of Los Angeles, connecting the bustling Hispanic marketplace on one side and the looming skyscrapers on Bunker Hill.

Preservationist-developer, Wayne Ratkovich, said, "Ira brings a passion to the job, an abiding love of cities and how they work." Yellin, himself, said, "I see Broadway as buildings being brought back to life, with full economic benefit for the owners, the merchants and the City. I don't want it to be [just] L.A.'s quaint piece of history." Now, nearly 25 years later, Grand Central Market continues to evolve to serve changing demographics and Yellin's vision of the catalytic effect of reinvigorated iconic properties on urban renewal has proven true. The intersection of Third and Broadway has been aptly dedicated as "Ira Yellin Square".

- Sandy Bleifer

Quotes extrapolated from numerous articles and papers courtesy of Downtown Properties and the Yellin Company.

500

EXIT

In the mid-1990s, artist Sandy Bleifer focused her attention on a pivotal moment in Los Angeles' contemporary history: the revitalization of downtown LA. Her first office as co-founder of Angels Walk LA was adjacent to the Bradbury Building and led her to turn her eye on all the historic buildings of downtown Los Angeles. As a Broker/Consultant/Commercial Real Estate Specialist, Bleifer worked on behalf of tenants and buyers, founding DownTown Enterprises in 1996 and later DownTown LA Realty. With a clear vision for a vibrant residential and business community in the neglected historic and industrial sections of downtown Los Angeles, she set about to convey that vision to those who had long disregarded the area.

The documentation of her activities and projects in these seminal years are archived in the University of Southern California's Southern California Studies, USC Libraries Special Collections. The Los Angeles Public Libraries have acquired her photographs.

Bleifer's artistic practice began with silkscreen, collage, and an exploration of paper: a continuing discovery into its complex nature and its ability to serve as a metaphor for the world around us. Early in her career as an exhibiting artist, social and political activism crept into the mix. Soon she began creating art installations that became a focus and galvanizing force for the reconsideration of major historical events: the Holocaust and the bombing of Hiroshima and Nagasaki.

In recent years, Bleifer's experience downtown has infused her art with a pro-active agenda using interactive installations, video, and community engagement.

photo by Gary Leonard

9 781733 071918